The Past in Question
Series Editor: J. F. Aylett

Life in Norman Times

David Whitehall

Edward Arnold
A division of Hodder & Stoughton
LONDON MELBOURNE AUCKLAND

Acknowledgements

The publishers would like to thank the following for their permission to reproduce copyright illustrations:
Cambridge University Library, pp 4, 10, 28 right, 39; British Museum, pp 6, 29 bottom; The Mansell Collection Ltd, p 7, 8, 9, 23, 35, 44; British Library, pp 11, 20, 27 bottom, 32, 36, 38 right; Bibliothèque Nationale, Paris, p 13. George Hall, pp 15, 21; Weidenfeld Publishers, p 18; Mary Evans Picture Library, pp 19, 24; Wayland Picture Library, p 20 left; Barnaby's, pp 22, 27 top, 29 right, 43; Public Record Office, pp 24 left, 40, 42; National Portrait Gallery, p 25; Aerofilms Ltd, pp 28 left, 47; Ron Boardman, p 29 top left; Bodleian Library, pp 31 top, 33 cover; Sotheby's, p 31 bottom; BBC Hulton Picture Library, p 46.

For Thérèse

Illustrations by Philip Page

First published in Great Britain 1989

British Library Cataloguing in Publication Data

Whitehall, David.
Life in Norman times.—(The Past in question).
1. England. Social life, 1066–1154—For schools
I. Title II. Series
942.02

ISBN 0 7131 8531 7

Typeset in 12 on 13 point Century Schoolbook by Butler & Tanner Ltd
Printed in Great Britain for Edward Arnold, the educational, academic and medical publishing division of Hodder and Stoughton Limited, Mill Road, Dunton Green, Sevenoaks, Kent
by Thomson Litho Ltd., East Kilbride, Scotland

Contents

1 Harold, King for a Year

The mourners moved slowly past the coffin of the dead king. Edward the Confessor, King of England, was dead. He had no children to replace him, and people wondered who would be the next king. They found out on the day of Edward's funeral. It was Harold, the dead king's brother-in-law.

The shouts echoed around the church, 'Long live the King.' But from this moment on, Harold was in danger. He had enemies who had sworn to get their revenge. One was his own brother, Tostig. The other was William, Duke of Normandy, and he was furious.

A *Harold crowns himself king in a 13th century painting.*

William said that Edward had promised him that he would be the next king. He also said that Harold had agreed to help him, and had now broken his promise. William wanted to make him sorry for this. He got ready to attack England, and fight Harold. Tostig did the same.

In September, Tostig landed in the north of England with the King of Norway and a large army. Harold was already waiting for William to attack in the south. He did not expect to be attacked in the north as well.

Harold marched from London with his army and fought the Norwegians at Stamford Bridge. There, he won a great victory. But his men were tired out after the long march and battle. Three days later, he heard that William had landed in the south.

Movements of the armies in the week before the Battle of Hastings.

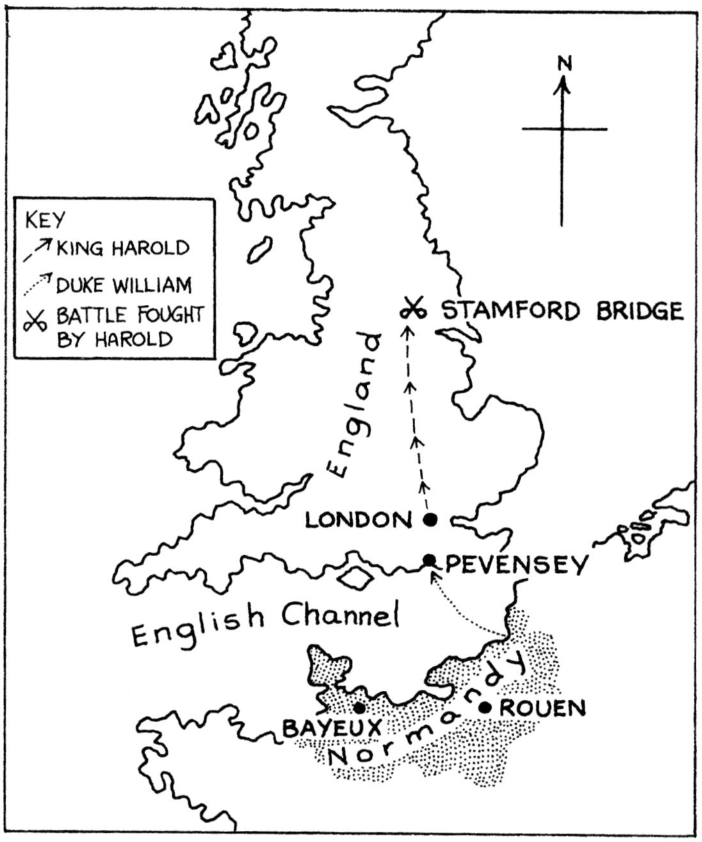

At this point, if you were Harold what would you do next?

1 March south straight away and attack William
2 Wait for two weeks until your army has recovered and then attack
3 Make peace with William and let him become king
4 Do nothing

Now, suppose you can travel back in time and interview Harold. What would you ask him? You could start by asking him if he was sad about his brother Tostig, who had been killed at Stamford Bridge. Later on, he might tell you if he really had broken a promise to William. Most important of all, you want to know what he is going to do next.

Harold tells you that he is going to march south straight away and attack William at Hastings. He has asked you to ride with him. The battle is about to begin. . . .

At the moment of course, time travel is just a dream. But safely back in the classroom, you can still find out what Harold was like. You can do it by reading what people have written about him. The trouble is that they do not all agree. And after reading the **sources** in this chapter, you might wonder if they are really about the same person.

When this happens, which writer do you believe? First you need to know *who* the writers were. From this you can start to work out *why* they do not agree.

Read these descriptions of Harold, and look closely at the people who wrote them.

B *Around 1130 an English* **monk** *called Florence of Worcester described Harold like this.*

As soon as Harold became king, he made it his job to stop unfair laws and make good ones. He was kind and polite to all good men, but strictly punished all criminals. He ordered the arrest of all thieves and robbers. He worked very hard to defend his country, by land, and at sea.

C *A Norman monk called Oderic Vitalis wrote this about Harold around 1135.*

Harold was guilty of lying, cruelty and wickedness. In the three months he had been king many people had been badly treated. He had no right to be king. Because of this, families now fought with each other and women were sad when their sons and husbands were killed.

D *Gurtha, Harold's other brother, advised him to wait before attacking William's army. This is what Harold did next, according to another writer.*

Harold was very angry. He ignored the good advice of his friends and swore at his brother. He lost his temper so badly that he even kicked his mother.

Activities

1 a) Draw the map in your book. On it, show Harold's journey to Hastings.
b) Look at the map. Harold is marching south straight after beating the Norwegians. Are his chances of beating William now better, or worse than they were?

2 Read source B, C and D. Copy this table in to your book and fill in Harold's good points and bad points.

	Good points	*Bad points*
1		
2		
3		

3 a) Read source C. Copy a new table and write down what this writer thinks about Harold.
b) Why do you think the writers of B and C disagree?

4 Do you think source D was written by a Norman or an Englishman? Give reasons for your answer.

5 a) Do you think the painter of source A saw Harold crown himself King? Give reasons.
b) How could you check that this event really took place?

2 The Battle of Hastings

A *A 15th century painting of the armies before the battle.*

On the afternoon of October 13, 1066, William's spies hurried to tell him the news. Harold was coming. That evening, Harold led his army to a hill about seven kilometres from Hastings. Throughout the south of England, men were marching to join him.

William knew he had to attack the next day even if it meant fighting uphill. So, at sunrise on October 14, the Norman army moved off.

Most of William's men were knights. They fought on horseback, using long spears and swords. By nine o'clock they had reached the hill. Above them stood 7000 English warriors.

According to one story, a poet spoke to both armies before the battle. When he had finished, the Norman archers stepped forward and shot their arrows. The English crouched behind their shields, waiting for William's foot soldiers to attack.

When they did, soldiers on both sides were cut to pieces in fierce hand-to-hand fighting. Then the knights charged. Each time they attacked, the English stood firm.

As the afternoon dragged on, the two armies became more tired. It was already getting dark when William began his last attack. This time it was successful. His knights surrounded Harold and the English soldiers who were left, and hacked them to death.

Most of the people who wrote about the battle afterwards were Normans. Because of this, you should expect their accounts to be different from those of English writers.

None of them saw the battle. They had to find out from soldiers who had fought in it. But they could have forgotten some of the facts. Or made some of them up. And few of the writers checked what they were told. So today you must not assume that their accounts give the whole truth.

In spite of these problems, the writers can still help us to find out about the battle. Some of them were alive when it happened. And whether they saw it or not, their accounts are called primary sources. Other people have written about the battle although they were not alive when it took place. Their accounts are called secondary sources.

Now, compare these primary and secondary sources about the Battle of Hastings.

B *A description of King Harold at the battle written by Florence of Worcester in the 12th century.*

He fought bravely from nine in the morning until night time. He defended himself with such courage that the enemy thought they would never beat him. But sadly, as it started to get dark, Harold was wounded and killed.

C *In 1071, William of Poitiers described what happened to Harold's body.*

Harold had no badges on him and could not be identified by his face, only by certain marks on his body. King William gave it to William Malet for burial, and not to Harold's mother. She wanted to bury Harold herself and offered William her son's weight in gold. But the King thought that it was wrong to get money in this way. He did not think that Harold should be buried as his mother wanted, because so many men had died because of his greed. He said jokingly that, because Harold had tried so hard to guard the coast of England, he should be buried by the sea shore.

D *Thousands of men and horses were killed during the battle.*

E *Around 1320, Matthew of Westminster also described what happened to Harold.*

At last Harold fell after his brain had been split through by an arrow. But while the King was still breathing, one of the Normans ran up to him and cut off his leg. William had him beaten for this, and expelled him from the army.

He sent the body of King Harold to his mother. William did not want the large **ransom** that she had offered for the body. When she received it, she buried it at Waltham in the church which Harold himself had built.

Activities

1 Put these parts of the Norman attack in the order in which they happened:
knights charged; archers shot their arrows; foot soldiers attacked.

2 a) Look at source D. Which soldier do you think is the Norman knight? Give reasons.
b) How were his weapons different from those of the English soldier?

3 Do you think source B was written by a Norman or an Englishman? Explain your answer.

4 a) Read sources C and E. Copy the questions below and fill in the answers given by these two writers.

	Source C	*Source E*
How was Harold killed?		
Who buried Harold?		
Where was Harold buried?		

b) William of Poitiers was King William's personal **priest**. Can you think of any reasons why he might not describe how Harold was killed?
c) What problems do you think there are with the evidence of Matthew of Westminster?

5 a) Look at source A. Explain in your own words what you think is happening.
b) Compare this picture with source D and the description of the battle given in this chapter. How is source A different?

3 The Bayeux Tapestry

Many stories have been told about the Battle of Hastings. According to one of them, Harold was not killed at all. He managed to escape from the battlefield and spent the rest of his life as a **hermit**.

People have argued about this and stories like it ever since the battle. And today, although historians can compare them with accounts that were written at the time, they cannot be certain about everything that happened. There is not enough **evidence**. It might help if they could study evidence that was actually taken from the battlefield. But so far nothing has been found.

It is also difficult to imagine what the battle was like. Fortunately we have the Bayeux **Tapestry** to help us. This tells the story of the Norman invasion and the Battle of Hastings in pictures. People think it was made for **Bishop** Odo, William's half-brother, by needleworkers in England.

The Bishop hung the tapestry in his church at Bayeux. He wanted the people who prayed there to see it, and to know why William had invaded England. There were facts that he thought were important and he wanted people to know about them.

He hoped they would tell their friends about King Edward's promise to William. About how he sent Harold to make that promise. And how Harold went back on his word and made himself king. The Bishop was pleased that so many people could see the tapestry. These people would know the Norman side of the story.

These are the pictures they saw. In five of them you can see words written in Latin. These are captions which explain what is happening.

Few of the people could read, but priests would explain to them what the words meant. Through these words and pictures they would have no doubt about why William invaded England. You can read the English translation of the captions underneath each picture.

A *William visits Guy and orders him to let Harold go. William pays Guy a large ransom.*

Guy leads Harold to William, Duke of the Normans.

B *Harold makes a promise to William. He puts his right hand on a box containing the bones of dead saints.*

Harold made an **oath** to William.

C *King Edward tells Harold to go and see William in Normandy.*

King Edward.

D *Harold helped William fight against Duke Conan of Brittany. William made Harold a knight. As one of William's knights, Harold had to do what William told him.*

Here William gave arms to Harold.

E *Harold's ship is blown off course. He lands on the coast of France but is held prisoner by Guy of Ponthieu, one of William's enemies.*

Here Guy arrests Harold.

F *Harold's brothers, Leofwine and Gurtha, were killed in the battle.*

Captions are important because they often give more information about the people in a picture. They can explain what the people are doing. And where pictures have been deliberately chosen to tell a story, captions can get the message over to people.

The Bayeux Tapestry shows how pictures and captions can be used to tell one side of a story. It is one that English writers do not agree with. For example, the monks who wrote the Anglo-Saxon **Chronicle**, which was completed in 1154, do not say that Harold went to see William. And even the tapestry does not tell us what kind of promise Harold made to William.

Historians cannot be certain of this, and many other parts of the story. There is simply not enough evidence.

G *This is written in the* Anglo-Saxon Chronicle. *It describes how William went to see King Edward in 1054.*

Count William came from overseas with a large army of Frenchmen. The King welcomed him, and many of his friends. Then William went home.

Activities

1 Look at the pictures from the Bayeux Tapestry. Then write down the captions in the correct order.

2 In source A which man do you think is Harold? Give reasons for your choice.

3 According to the tapestry, what reasons did William have for being angry with Harold?

4 Look at the bottom of source F. Write down one reason why historians cannot study evidence from the battlefield itself.

5 Why do you think the Anglo-Saxon Chronicle does not mention Harold's visit to William?

6 a) Read source G. Why might William have gone to see King Edward in 1054?
b) Do you think source G backs up William's claim to be king, or Harold's?

7 Draw the scene where William meets King Edward. Make your picture like the ones from the Bayeux Tapestry. Underneath it, write a caption from the Norman point of view.

4 The Monks Who Wrote About William

Today, you can listen to news on the radio and watch it on television. You can read about it in newspapers. The news will be from all parts of the world.

In Norman times, most people knew little about what was happening beyond their own village. And it could be many days before they heard about a war or the death of a king.

Some people knew what was happening, though. They were the monks who wrote down what they had seen and heard in chronicles. From them, we can learn about the people and places that were making the news.

But there are problems with the chronicles, as with all written evidence. The writers do not always agree. And some are biased because they only give one side of the story.

You may have heard the word *biased* used in sport. It is a word that is often used to describe a referee who is being unfair to one side. The word has a similar meaning when it is used by historians.

A monk at his writing desk.

A *William of Jumièges gives a copy of his book* The Dukes of Normandy *to King William.*

When William invaded England, he brought with him writers he could trust. They were Normans like him. He knew they would write about the conquest, and tell people that it was a good thing.

Most of the writers were monks. They were pleased with William. While he was king, the Church became very powerful. He built churches and **monasteries** all over England. The monasteries owned a quarter of all the land and were very rich. So, the monks had reasons for being biased in William's favour.

Before writing about him, the monks thought carefully about the words they would use. They wanted people to think he was a good king. So, they used words like 'brave' and 'strong' to describe him. In the stories they told, William was 'fair' and 'honest'.

Words like these show what the monks thought about William. They liked him and didn't always mention his bad points. The English writers did. Their country had been attacked and King Harold had been killed. They thought William was a bad king and told people so.

When writers cannot agree, you must decide which one to believe. First, find out who they were. This might explain *why* a writer is biased. Then compare what they have written with the accounts of other people. Look closely for any facts that have been left out. This can show *how* a writer is biased.

Then check the words in the accounts. The writers may well have chosen them for a reason, perhaps to make you believe something that was not totally true.

B *This is an extract from William of Jumièges' book. It describes what William did after the Battle of Hastings.*

This brave Duke, after following and slaughtering his enemies, came back to the battlefield in the middle of the night. At first dawn he took the road to London. At length this lord of battle brought his soldiers safely across the River Thames.

From there he marched on London. The Londoners gave **hostages** and gave themselves and all that they owned to their lord and most noble conqueror.

His victory was complete after so many dangers. I cannot praise his wonderful virtues high enough.

C *Paintings can mislead people too. This one of William was painted in the 13th century.*

D *Around 1135 Oderic Vitalis described some of the writers that William knew.*

They knew his secrets, and by his kindness, they got wealth and power that they could never have hoped for.

E *In the 12th century a monk wrote this:*

Earl William built castles throughout the country and made the poor people unhappy. After that, things got much worse.

Activities

1 Explain the meaning of the word *biased.*

2 Look at source A and read the caption. Do you think that William of Jumièges' evidence might be biased for or against the king? Explain your answer.

3 a) Read source B. Make a list of the words or phrases which you think give a good picture of William.
b) Write out the passage, but do NOT include the biased words.
c) Do you think your passage would give people a different opinion about William? Give reasons.

4 Read source D. Do you think this would affect what some people wrote about the king? Explain your answer.

5 Look at source C. Why do you think the painter has shown William holding this model rather than a sword or dagger?

6 Do you think source E was written by a Norman or an Englishman? Give reasons.

7 Monks used to start their writing with a capital letter like the one in source A. Choose another letter of the alphabet, and draw it as you think the monks would have done.

5 The Feudal System

On Christmas Day, 1066, William was crowned King of England. The Norman **barons** who had helped him now waited for their reward. They wanted land. And because many of the English **nobles** were dead, or had fled abroad, there was a lot to spare. William gave some of it to the barons.

He had to protect the barons if England was attacked. In turn, the barons had to look after the knights. And the knights protected the villeins.

For the king, this system had risks. He had to make sure the barons could not use their soldiers to gang up on him.

In return, they had to make two promises – that they would always be loyal to him, and that they would find soldiers to fight for him if there was a war.

The barons gave some of their land to the knights. The knights shared out most of it with the **villeins** who farmed the land. And every man swore an oath of loyalty to their lord, the person who had given them the land. This was called 'making homage'.

Apart from this, everyone agreed to do certain duties for their lord. This bargain between people – of land for duties – is called the Feudal System.

Under this system, the chief lord was the king. He owned all the land. But he had a duty, too. So he gave each baron small pieces of land in different parts of the country. This made it difficult for the barons to get an army together.

There was another risk, too. The barons gave land to their knights. To get it, the knights had to promise that they would be loyal to the barons. But if a baron went against the king, his knights would have to decide who they would fight for – the king or the baron. William solved this problem by making every knight take a special oath of loyalty to him.

In Norman times, just like today, people could be fined for breaking the law. William allowed the barons and knights to keep some of these fines. And if a villein did not do all his lord's duties, he could be fined as well.

A *This 13th century picture shows knights making homage to their king.*

B *In Norman times, anyone who received land took one of these oaths:*

I become your man from this day forward, for life and limb and loyalty. I shall be true and faithful to you for the lands I hold from you.

I become your man and I will be loyal to you with my life and limbs above all other men.

C *From the* Domesday Book, *1086:*

Adam Underwood of Brailes, Warwickshire, holds thirty **acres** of his lord, the Earl of Warwick, and in return he has to give the following dues and services:

1 Work every Monday, Wednesday and Friday from October to August.
Work two days a week from August to October. This can be ploughing, haymaking, harvesting, carting stones and gathering nuts.
2 Leave his own land at hay making and harvest time and work for his lord.
3 Make gifts of oats, a hen and food for three horses, 12d at Christmas, one penny for every pig over a year old, and half a penny for younger ones.

Aluric, **sheriff** of Huntingdon, had a house in the time of King Edward, which William took and afterwards gave to his wife and sons.

D

No. of English nobles who owned land		No. of Norman barons who owned land	
1065	1086	1065	1086
180	2	0	178

E *This is taken from the* Romsley Manor Court Rolls, *1294.*

Matilda and Margery de Kelmestowe are in the habit of carting off the lord's wood. Clement Kelmestowe is convicted of taking away a cartload of brushwood. Fine 3d.

Activities

1 Write out this paragraph, filling in the gaps.

The Norman barons wanted________for helping William to win the Battle of Hastings. William gave them some. In return, the barons had to take an oath of________to the king. The barons gave some of their land to the________. They shared out most of it with the________. Every man who was given land had to do________to the lord who had given it them. This is called the________System.

2 a) Look at source A. Which man do you think is the king?
b) What do you think is happening?

3 If the king in source A was William, which oath in source B would the knights take? Give reasons for your choice.

4 Look at source C. Which of the villein's duties do you think was most annoying to him, and why?

5 a) In source C, do you think Aluric was an Englishman or a Norman? Explain why.
b) Look at source D. How many English nobles owned land in 1086? How does source C help to explain why this was?

6 Read source E. What do you think the Kelmestowes would use the stolen wood for?

6 The Siege of Exeter, 1068

Many people did not want William to be their king.

When William was crowned king, the people who lived around London were pleased. They came out to watch him ride through the streets. But in other parts of the country, people were not pleased at all. They had liked Harold and did not want William to be their king. Now they made plans to fight against him.

For the next two years, William struggled to keep control of England. One of his first battles was with the people of Exeter. Many of Harold's friends lived there and William was determined that they should accept him as king. He arrived outside the town walls with a large army.

We do not know for certain what happened next, even though many people saw it happen and at least three people wrote about it. They all agree that in 1068 William marched to Exeter. The people living there refused to open the gates. He then attacked the town until the people gave in.

William won the **siege**. The writers all agree about this. But there are many things about it that they do not agree on. And each one of them has written things about the siege that the others have not mentioned.

To understand why this is, you need to check who the writers were. This has already helped you to explain why people wrote such different accounts about Harold. Now it can help you decide why these writers do not agree about the siege. From it, you can also see why they might not tell the whole truth about what happened.

Suppose one of the writers knew all the facts but deliberately missed some of them out. His account would only tell people part of the story about the siege. From this, people might get the idea that it was a good thing that William had won it.

Perhaps the writer wanted them to believe this. But because they did not have all the facts, people would not be able to decide this for themselves. They would have to take the writer's word for it.

The town walls of Exeter, built in Norman times.

On this page, there are three accounts of the siege. They all give facts about what happened during it, but not all of them explain why it happened. Decide for yourself why the people of Exeter did not want William as their king.

A *An English monk wrote this in the* Anglo-Saxon Chronicle:

The king imposed a heavy **tax** on the miserable people and destroyed everything that he overran. Then he went to Devonshire and besieged the city of Exeter for 18 days. But he had made fair promises to them, and carried them out badly.

B *The English monk William of Malmesbury wrote this in the 1120's:*

With God's help, the king easily conquered the city of Exeter when it **rebelled**. Part of the wall fell down accidentally and this made an opening for him. He attacked it very fiercely because one of the men standing on the wall had bared his bottom and broken wind in front of the Normans.

C *Oderic Vitalis wrote this in about 1135:*

When the leaders (of Exeter) heard that the king's army was getting near, they went out to meet him. They promised to obey all his commands and they gave hostages to the king. But when they returned to their fellow citizens, they found that they would not give in. The king was very angry when he heard this news.

He rode up to the gates and found that they were shut. Crowds of people stood on the city walls. The king ordered the whole army to move to the city. Then one of the hostages had his eyes put out in front of the gates.

The king attacked the city on all sides for many days. In the end, the leaders were forced to ask for mercy. They went out to meet the king with pretty young women and priests carrying bibles. They lay down at the king's feet and the king forgave them. The people of Exeter were full of joy and thanked God.

Activities

1 Put these events in the order in which they happened:
the leaders met the king with women and priests; a hostage had his eyes put out; William marched with his army to Exeter; the king made people pay a heavy tax; crowds of people stood on the walls.

2 Read source A. Do you think that the writer feels sorry for the people of Exeter? How can you tell?

3 Which source makes William sound a fair king? Explain your answer.

4 a) Compare sources A and C. Source A gives facts about the siege that C does not. What are they?
b) Why do you think Oderic Vitalis, who was a Norman writer, has not mentioned them?

5 Why do you think the king put out the eyes of the hostage in front of the gates?

6 Which source is least useful to you in explaining what happened at the siege of Exeter? Give reasons for your answer.

7 Norman Castles

William did not take revenge on the people of Exeter. Instead, he ordered them to build a castle at the highest point of the town. In it, he put soldiers ready to deal with any troublemakers. From all parts of the town, people could see the castle. It reminded them of what would happen if anyone went against William.

He told his barons to build castles on the land he had given them. Most of the English had never seen a castle before. They got used to seeing them, though. In the ten years after William's invasion, they had to build forty.

Castles like these were quick and cheap to build. Later, when the Normans had better control over England, they built stone castles called keeps instead. Here the barons lived with their families and servants, and the soldiers who guarded the local people.

Many keeps are still standing today and the one in London is over thirty metres high. If there isn't one in your town, look out for street names like Castle Gate, Castle Hill or Castle Street. They might be a clue that there used to be a Norman castle somewhere nearby.

How a motte and bailey castle was made.

A castle under siege

A *There are few written accounts of castles being attacked. But this one, written by John Froissart in 1340, describes one way of doing it.*

Sir William Douglas and his companions bought a supply of oats, coal and straw and quietly sailed to a harbour near Edinburgh. They landed, then set off under cover of darkness taking ten or twelve of their trustiest men. These they dressed in tattered coats and hats to look like poor **merchants**. They loaded twelve ponies with sacks full of the supplies. Then the others set an ambush at the foot of the castle.

At daybreak, the merchants set out towards the castle with their horses. When they were on the slope, Sir William went in front and told the **porter** at the gatehouse that they had supplies to sell. The porter said that the goods were needed, but it was too early for him to dare and wake his lord up. So he told them to come forward and opened the gate of the bailey.

Sir William noticed that the porter had all the other keys of the castle gate. He cunningly asked him which key opened it. When the first gate was opened, the merchants took their ponies inside and unloaded two bags of coal so that the bailey gate would not shut.

Then they seized the porter and killed him very quietly. They took the keys and unlocked the castle gate. Then Sir William blew on his horn and the others hidden in ambush rushed out towards the castle. The horn woke the castle guard, but it was too late.

Activities

1 a) This list describes how a motte and bailey castle was made by the English. Write it out in the correct order.

They dug a ditch around a large bailey.
On top of this, they built a wooden castle.
They dug a large ditch.
They threw the earth into the middle to make a mound, or motte.

b) Explain why the Normans built their first castles out of wood, and later of stone.

2 a) Read the first paragraph of source A. What fact in the story is the writer not certain of?
b) How could you check the other parts of the story?

3 Explain what you would have done if you had been the porter of Edinburgh Castle.

4 Imagine you have just invented one of the siege weapons in the picture above. Write a letter to King William I explaining how it works. Draw a picture of it to help you.

8 The 'Harrying of the North'

After the siege of Exeter, King William wondered how many other towns would go against him. He ordered more castles to be built and everywhere forced the local people to obey.

Already people were angry at the high taxes that they had to pay. Worse still, they might be attacked and robbed by Norman soldiers. The soldiers were rarely caught and never punished.

But not everyone gave in. Those who didn't hid in woods and other lonely places. Here they waited, and secretly murdered any Normans whom they found.

Attacks like these annoyed William. But he was more worried by news from the north of England. The people there did not want him as king and were ready to fight. To make matters worse, King Sweyn of Denmark had agreed to help them. And in September 1069, 300 ships packed with Danish soldiers arrived.

A *The Danes sailed in ships like this one.*

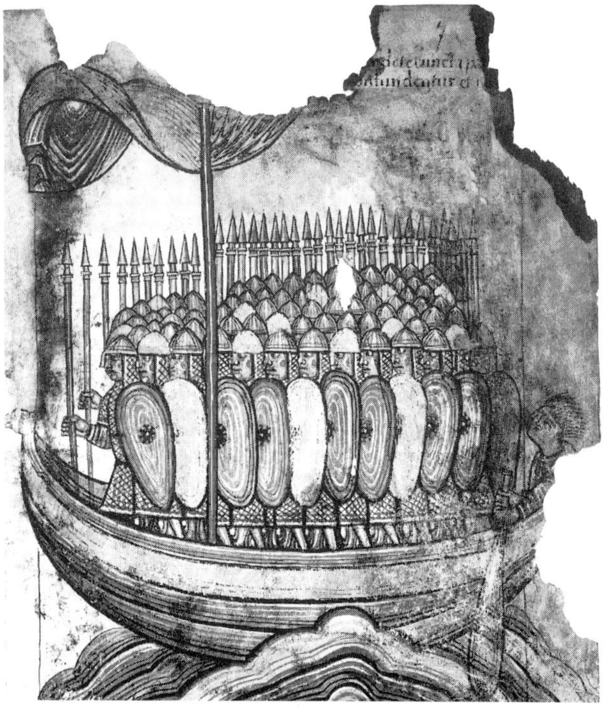

Near the River Humber, they met up with the English army. Their target was York. A week later, they had captured the castle and set fire to the town.

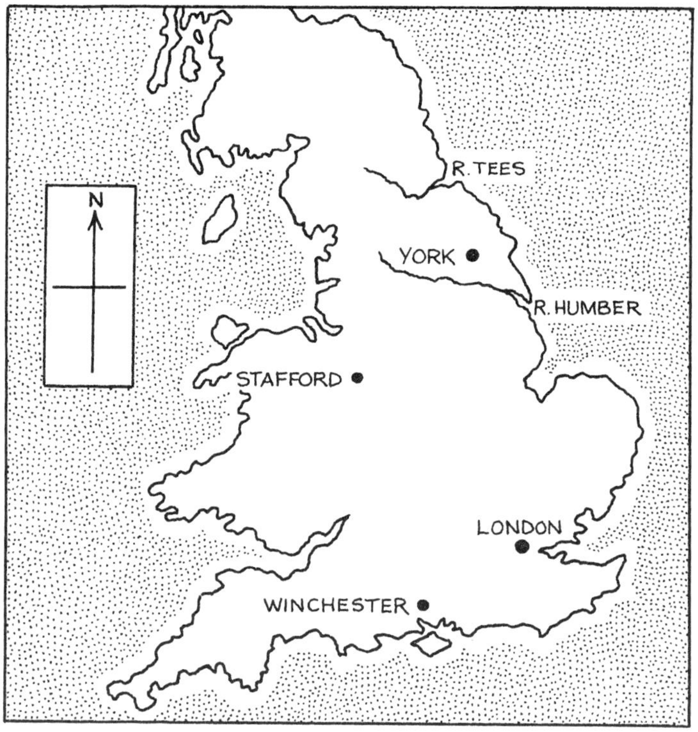

William quickly got his army together. He had been staying at Winchester. And from there, he marched north. His first stop was the River Humber. He wanted to catch the Danish soldiers before they got back to their ships.

But he was too late. The soldiers had gone. They were sailing up and down the coast, waiting to see what William would do next.

He marched south and stopped a **revolt** in Staffordshire. Then he went back to the River Humber. The Danish army had landed again, and gone north to the River Tees. William did the same and, for a week, the two armies marched across northern England.

They never met. This time William could not risk a fight. He knew that if he lost, he would not be King of England. And like Harold before him, he might also be killed. So, he followed the Danish army until finally they gave up and went home.

On Christmas Eve, William led his army into York. He was safe. But people in the north had wanted to get rid of him. Some of them had fought on the Danish side. Now he made them pay for this.

In January 1070, William marched again through the north of England. People never forgot what he did next. Years later they called it 'The Harrying of the North.'

B *Around 1135 Oderic Vitalis wrote this:*

He marched through country overgrown with woods, intending to catch the enemy. They fell under his sword. He wasted their lands and burnt their houses with everything in them. Never did William commit so much cruelty. To his lasting disgrace, he ordered the corn and cattle and all the farm tools to be collected in heaps and set on fire.

He destroyed the land north of the Humber. There followed a severe **famine** which caused the innocent population so much misery that more than 100,000 people died.

C *This picture is taken from the Bayeux Tapestry. It shows what happened to people in many parts of England after the Battle of Hastings.*

D *An English monk called Henry of Huntingdon wrote this account early in the 12th century:*

In the whole country there was famine. People were so hungry that they ate human flesh, as well as horses, dogs and cats. Some people became slaves to try and stay alive. Others left their country, but fell down in the middle of the journey and died.

It was horrific to see human corpses decaying in the houses and roads, and swarming with worms. There was a terrible smell, because no one was left to bury them, all having been killed by the sword or by the famine.

For nine years, no one lived in the villages between York and Durham. They became places where wild animals and robbers lurked, and they were a great danger to travellers.

Activities

1 Copy the map into your book. On it, show the route William took between 1069 and 1070.

2 Make a list of the reasons people had for disliking William.

3 Read source B. Do you think the writer agrees or disagrees with what William did? Explain your answer.

4 What problems are there with Henry of Huntingdon's account?

5 a) Look at source C. What are the English people doing in the picture?
b) Do you think it shows a fair fight? Give at least three reasons for your answer.
c) Look at the bottom of source C. What do you think happened to the people who ran away?

6 Which of these reasons do you think best explains why William burnt the farmland in the north?
a) He was a cruel king.
b) He wanted to make sure that if the Danish king invaded again, his soldiers could not get food.
c) He wanted to try a new type of farming.
Give reasons for your choice.

7 Look at the ship in source A. How is it different from a modern ship?

8 Design a front cover for a book called *The Harrying of the North.*

9 The Church in Norman England

After the 'Harrying of the North', King William had control of most of England. Now he could organise the country as he wanted. Englishmen who had done important jobs before the invasion were sacked and Normans put in their places.

First to go were the bishops who led the Church. The king gave their jobs to his friends and relations. He had to make sure that the Church was run by men he could trust. Now, priests up and down the country would tell people to lead good, honest lives and obey the new king.

Everywhere, English churches were pulled down and replaced by huge, Norman churches. To local people, they were a permanent reminder of their new rulers.

There was a church in every village. Tapestries and stained glass windows made them look very colourful inside. These showed scenes from the bible stories. They helped people understand the church services which were in Latin.

Few people could understand Latin, but they got the message from the pictures of heaven and hell on the walls. These left people in no doubt about what might happen to them.

A *A painting like those found on the walls of Norman churches.*

Monks spent much of their day praying.

Most people died before they were forty. Sickness and disease made sure of that. Or if the harvest was poor, people died of starvation. Thousands more died fighting in battle. So people worried about dying. The village priest helped comfort them. He said that if they were good they would go to heaven, and people believed him.

For some men religion was more important than anything else in life. These were the monks. They thought they could only live a Christian life away from other people.

They went to live in a monastery and spent much of their day praying to God. Women who thought this way became nuns and lived in nunneries.

Rich people gave money to the monasteries, hoping that their prayers would be answered.

The monasteries owned land as well so they were very powerful. William made sure they were run his way. He chose the **abbots**. Most of them were Norman. He allowed them to make many changes in their monasteries.

In 1083 Thurstan, the abbot of Glastonbury Abbey, forced his monks to sing Norman hymns. The monks wanted to sing the English ones that they were used to.

Glastonbury Abbey.

B *This is what happened next, according to an English monk writing in about 1150:*

Abbot Thurstan was not wise and did not look after his monks properly. They complained and politely asked him to treat them better. The monks said that if he treated them fairly they would be loyal and obedient to him. But the abbot did nothing of the sort. He treated them badly and threatened them with worse.

One day the abbot went into the **chapter** and shouted at the monks. Then he sent for some knights who came into the monastery fully armed. The monks were afraid and did not know what to do.

Some of them went into the church and locked the doors. But the knights broke in, and threw missiles at the monks who were standing near the altar. Some of the knights went upstairs and fired arrows down on them. The monks crept under the altar and prayed to God because these men would not show them mercy. The knights killed three monks and wounded eighteen in the church. Their blood flowed from the altar on to the steps, and from the steps on to the floor.

C *A description of hell written by an English monk in about 1050.*

There were trees on fire, and sinners being tortured on those trees. Some were hung by their feet, some by their hair and some by the arm. There was a furnace of fire burning with seven flames, and many sinners were punished in it. It had a fiery wheel which was turned a thousand times every day by an evil angel. At each turn a thousand sinners were burnt on it.

Kilpeck Church, Herefordshire.

Activities

1 Why do you think William sacked the English bishops and replaced them with Normans?

2 a) Read source B. Does it make Thurstan sound like a good or a bad abbot? Explain why you think this.
b) What other evidence would help you check this writer's story about the knights' attack?

3 Imagine you are one of the Glastonbury monks. From your point of view, describe Abbot Thurstan and the attack by the knights in your monastery.

4 a) Do you think source A is a picture of heaven or hell? Explain how you decided.
b) Describe what is happening in the picture.
c) Read source C. Use this to draw your own picture of hell.

10 Hereward the Wake

In one part of England people still tried to hold out against William. They lived in the Fenlands of East Anglia. Here the land is flat and many streams and rivers flow through it. In Norman times you could look for miles and see nothing but swamps and small islands.

Today, much of the water has been drained away and roads have been built. But for the large army that King William brought there in 1071, it was a dangerous place. His soldiers didn't know the secret tracks through the swamps. They could easily be sucked in and drowned.

They had come to capture the island of Ely, and the last of the English rebels. For months people had been sailing from this island to attack Norman farms and villages. They were led by Hereward the Wake. He was a nobleman whose land had been taken from him by the Normans.

In later years, people who had never met Hereward told stories about his bravery – how he could fight six men at once with the sword he called Brainbiter and how his horse Swallow was faster than any other.

A *The Fenlands today.*

Map of the Isle of Ely.

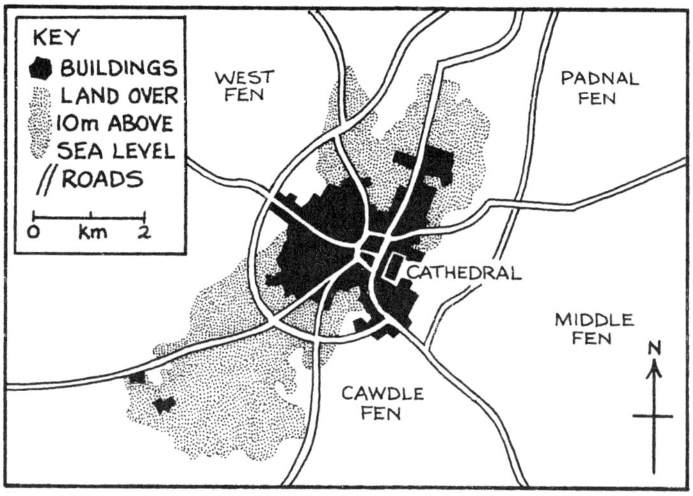

People believed these stories. But just like the stories of Robin Hood, they are legends for which historians have no evidence. So it is unlikely that the stories are true. But historians can be sure that Hereward was a real person. Accounts that were written by people at the time prove this.

They describe how in 1070 Hereward robbed Peterborough monastery with the help of Danish soldiers. The king was very angry about this. After the 'Harrying of the North', he did not think the Danes would try and return. Now Hereward had invited them back.

Next year William led an army into the Fens. He was going to stop Hereward once and for all. According to one story, he ordered a causeway to be built across the marshes to the Isle of Ely.

It wasn't strong enough, and when William's men crowded on to it the causeway sank. Hundreds of Norman soldiers drowned in the mud. Years later people said they saw skeletons in rusty armour being dragged out by local fishermen.

William then set up a wooden tower with a witch on top of it. She had to shout curses and make spells over Hereward's men. But in the night, they crept out and burnt the tower and the witch as well.

At last, William found a way on to the island. Some people said that the monks of Ely betrayed Hereward and showed the king a secret track. Again, there is no evidence for this. We know that somehow Hereward managed to escape. What happened to him afterwards, no one really knows.

B *An extract from the* Anglo-Saxon Chronicle, *written about 1120.*

In 1070 Danish soldiers came to Ely. English people from all the Fenlands joined them. Then the monks of Peterborough heard that Hereward and his men were going to rob their monastery. They said he was going to do this because the king had made a Frenchman called Turold the new abbot.

Before dawn, a monk went to see the abbot. He asked him to protect the monks. Next morning the outlaws came with many ships. They wanted to enter the monastery but the monks opposed them and they could not get in. Then they set fire to it and burnt down all the monks' houses.

The monks came to them and asked for a truce, but they paid no attention. They went into the monastery and took so much money and treasure that no man could count it up. These men said they were doing it out of loyalty to the monastery. Then they sailed to Ely where they put all the treasure.

Then came Abbot Turold and 160 Frenchmen with him, all fully armed. When he arrived he found everything burnt inside and out except the church.

C *Hereward attacks the Normans. The picture was painted in the 19th century.*

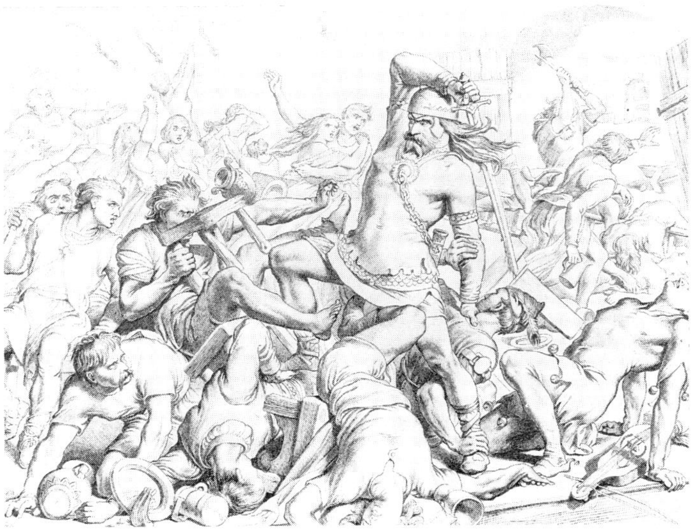

D *An account of William's attack written by a monk from Peterborough around 1120.*

He called out the fleet and his army and surrounded the land. He built a bridge over the River Ouse and went over it to the island. The fleet of ships stayed on the side towards the sea. And then all the outlaws surrendered except Hereward and those who wanted to be with him. He bravely led them out of the Fens. The king took weapons and ships and many treasures. He dealt with the men as he pleased.

E *A description of Ely written at the end of the 11th century.*

It is well known for its deer, and it has many flocks of sheep and herds of cow. In the water, hundreds of eels are caught, also pike, perch and roach. Many people say that salmon are also caught there, and the royal fish, the sturgeon. There one can find ducks and geese more than a man can count.

Activities

1 Read source B. Why did Hereward and his men rob Peterborough monastery? Do you believe the reason they gave?

2 Look at source A. Describe the problems that William would have in attacking land like this.

3 a) Is source C a primary or secondary source? Explain how you decided.
b) Does source C give the impression that Hereward was a hero or a villain? Give reasons.

4 a) Read source D. How did William manage to capture the island?
b) What do you think that William did to those men who surrendered?
c) Would you have done the same? Give reasons.

5 a) Read source E. Why do you think William did not try to lay siege to the island?
b) Use source E to design a travel poster for the island so that more Normans will come and stay there.

11 The Domesday Book

Great Domesday and Little Domesday – the two parts of Domesday Book.

In 1066 William had invaded England with a huge Norman army. Twenty years later he ordered an even larger army to set sail from France. This time it was not to attack. William needed it to defend England.

It was August 1085. King Cnut of Denmark had joined forces with Count Robert of Flanders. They were waiting with their armies for the right moment to invade.

William took this threat very seriously. He had been staying in Normandy when he heard the news. Now he returned to England. He took with him the largest army that had ever set sail. And according to one story, the English Channel was filled with ships stretching from coast to coast.

William ordered that crops in all coastal areas should be destroyed. People who lived near the coast had to leave their houses. For the barons the situation was not much better. They had to feed and house these people on their estates. All through the winter they waited for the invasion. It never came.

At last King William sent his army back to France. It had been very expensive to keep. People wondered who would pay for it. So did William.

For years people had paid taxes to the king according to the amount of land that they owned. This was how the king got his money. But he had never really known how much land people had, or how much they should pay in taxes.

At Christmas 1085, he announced a plan to find out. Teams of officials would visit every manor in the country. In each one they would find out how many people lived there, how much land they owned and how much tax they paid. They would even ask how many pigs, cows and sheep each villein had. They had seven months to find out.

In January 1086, the first officials set off. They were followed a few weeks later by a second group of officials. They checked all the answers to see if anyone had lied. There were severe punishments for anyone who had. People could be fined or forced to plunge their right hands in boiling water.

A *William I from the Bayeux Tapestry.*

All the answers were written down on **parchment** and made into a book. For William these answers were very interesting. Many people owned much more land than he had realised. So they weren't paying enough taxes. With this book, he could make sure that people paid the right amount in future.

B *William I by an unknown 16th century artist.*

It was called The Domesday Book. The word 'Domesday' meant 'The Day of Judgement.' The day God decided who went to heaven and who went to hell. On that day no one would argue with God's decisions. Just as no one would argue with what was written in the Domesday Book.

But what was William himself like? Writers have always disagreed about him. But so too have painters. In this chapter you can check some of their evidence to try and make up your own mind.

C *A description of William written by a Norman monk in about 1091.*

This king was wiser than any other prince. He was strong and tall but not clumsy. He never ate or drank too much. He hated drunkenness in all men and after his meal, he rarely drank more than three times.

D *This is the Domesday account for one village – Great Faringdon in Berkshire.*

The king holds Great Faringdon. Harold held it. Then it was assessed at 30 **hides**. Now it does not pay tax. There is land for 15 ploughs. The king has land for 3 ploughs. 27 villeins have 10 ploughs. There are 10 slaves. A mill with a fishery is worth 35 shillings. 130 acres of meadow; woodland for fencing. In this manor Alfsi has 4 hides and has land for 2 ploughs. Value of Great Faringdon before 1066 £16; later £12. Now £21 6s 8d.

Activities

1 a) Why did William order the Domesday Book to be made?
b) Look at source D. Who owned Great Faringdon in 1066?
c) Why did this village not pay any tax?
d) Suggest a reason why the land was worth more in 1086.

2 Only a few places in Wales and Scotland are mentioned in the Domesday Book. What does this tell you about King William's control of these countries?

3 a) Is source B a primary or a secondary source? Explain your answer.
b) List the differences you can see between source B and source A. Then make a list of things that are similar.
c) Which source do you think is most likely to show what William looked like? Give reasons.

4 a) Is source C a primary or a secondary source? Give reasons.
b) Why might this source be biased in favour of William?
c) According to the monk William was tall. Can you find out if this was true from sources A and B? Explain your answer.

12 Laxton, a Norman Village

Plan of Laxton.

In 1086, Laxton in Nottinghamshire was one of the many villages visited by officials in the Domesday Survey. Geoffrey Anselin owned Laxton. He was a baron and he decided who lived in the village, and who worked in the three open fields around it.

They were called open fields because they had no hedges or fences round them. Instead, they were divided into strips, which had earth banks or ditches in between them.

The strips were shared out, so that everyone in Laxton had some strips in each of the fields. In this way, everyone had a share of the good land and the bad land around the village. You can still see the open fields in Laxton today. They have hardly changed since Norman times.

The villeins could usually grow enough food for themselves. Just to make sure, they said a prayer over the land each spring. Or sometimes they left offerings of bread in the fields when ploughing started.

They used oxen to plough the land and it was a long, slow job. Work started as soon as it was light. The oxen were driven to one of the open fields and there they were tied to the plough.

It took two villeins to work the oxen. One stayed at the back to guide the plough through the soil. The other walked alongside the oxen. Sometimes this job was done by a villein's wife. She made sure the oxen went in a straight line by prodding them with a stick.

If it rained, they could be up to their knees in mud, and they would have to drag the oxen forward. It was worse when the weather was cold. The villeins were poor and their clothes were not warm enough to stop them shivering. Some didn't have shoes, and cut their feet on the frozen ground.

On days like this, they might wish they'd stayed in bed. They didn't dare do this, though. They knew that if their lord found out he would be very angry with them. So, for the rest of the day, they followed the oxen and ploughed their lord's strips.

It was only at weekends that the villeins could work on their own land. And source A shows the kind of rules they had to obey.

A *The by-laws of an Oxfordshire village, 1293.*

1 No one shall enter the fields with a cart to carry grain after sunset.
2 No one shall enter the fields except at the village entrances.
3 All grain collected in the fields shall be taken out openly through the middle of the town and not secretly by back ways.

A by-law of Newton Longville, 1290.
No one shall allow his animals to graze in any piece of cultivated land before his neighbour's crops have been harvested. If anyone is found doing this, he shall give the lord 6d. If anyone is found doing this at night, he shall give the lord 12d.

B *An extract from* Piers Ploughman *written by William Langland around 1350.*

'I have no penny,' said Piers, 'to buy chickens
Nor geese nor piglets, but I have two green cheeses
A few curds and cream and oat cake
And two loaves of beans and bran to bake
for my little ones.
And besides, I have no bacon, nor little eggs.
I have parsley and leeks and many cabbages.'

C *Today, tractors have made ploughing much easier, as the picture on the right shows.*

D *Villeins ploughing.*

Activities

1 Copy out and complete this paragraph.

There were three________around Laxton. They did not have________or fences round them. Instead, they were divided up into________and shared out amongst the________. Each year they grew crops in________of the fields. The other was not used at all and lay________.

2 a) Here are five things that the villeins in source C might grumble about: not having enough food; having to plough their lord's strips; the cold weather; getting up early; not having enough wood for the fire. Put these complaints in order of importance to the villeins. Give reasons for your top choice.

b) Look at sources B and D. Imagine you can hear what the villeins are saying. Write down their conversation.

3 List the differences you can see between source C and source D.

4 a) Look at source A. Why do you think the villeins made these rules?

b) Look at sources B and D. Imagine you can the laws at night were higher than in the day time?

13 Farming – How Else Can We Find Out?

Over the centuries, much of the evidence about Norman farms and villages has been destroyed. Roads and motorways now cut through what were once open fields. And land that once belonged to a lord of the manor is now covered by highrise flats and factory chimneys.

But in many parts of Britain it is still possible to find out where these villages stood. There are sources which can help you do this. You can read about some of them in this chapter.

Soil marks

Standing in a field, you probably wouldn't know if important buildings had once stood there. This is because the remains of walls and ditches are buried under the soil. But from an aeroplane, they show up because the soil above them is a different colour.

A *Soil marks photographed from an aeroplane.*

Photographs of these soil marks can tell us about the size of old villages. On the ground, they also show where historians should look for other clues.

Ridge and furrow

In many fields, there are long ridges with hollows in between them. They were made by ploughs hundreds of years ago.

When the villeins ploughed up the field, they turned the soil to the right and into the middle of the strip. At the top of the field they turned the plough and went down it.

B *Aerial photograph of Lower Ditchford, Warwickshire, a deserted Norman village.*

By the end of the day, this would have made a long ridge of soil. On either side of it would be two furrows where the plough blades had cut. Because the villeins ploughed in the same place each year, the furrows became quite deep. Again, these can be better seen from an aeroplane. The soil is dark along the furrow, where the rain water has sunk in, and lighter above the ridge.

Pollen

Each summer, some people suffer from hay fever. It might seem strange, but the pollen which causes it can also help us to work out what the countryside was like in Norman times.

You might have seen pollen in a plant or sticking to the body of a bee. It is a yellow powder which is made up of tiny grains. Some of these help to make other trees and plants. The rest fall to the ground. Over the years they are covered by rotting plants and soil.

Pollen grain.

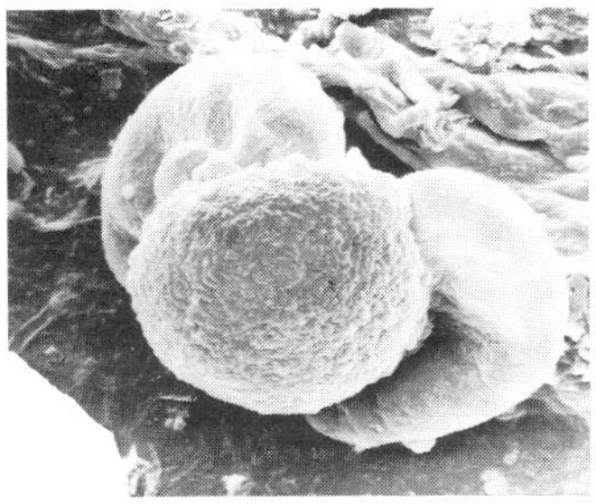

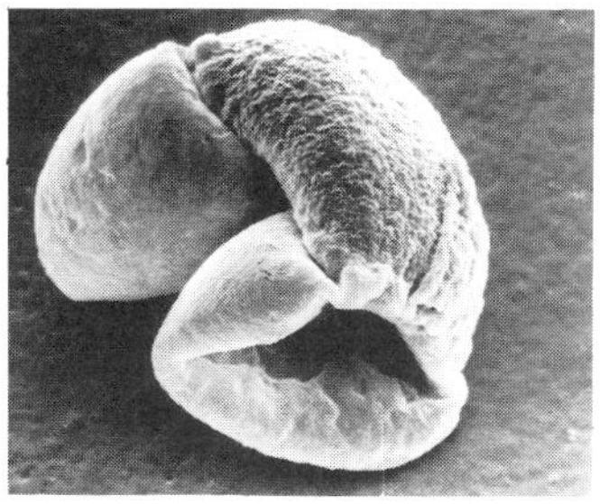

Suppose you dug up soil from around your school, and then counted the pollen grains in it under a microscope. If the grains were mostly from trees, the land was once probably covered by woods. If most of the grains came from wild grasses or **bracken**, it was probably moorland.

Animal bones

Another way of checking whether there was once a village nearby is to look for animal bones in the soil. Most villeins owned a pig. Some might have a cow or a few goats to provide milk and meat. After eating the animals, the villeins threw away any remaining bones and eventually these would be covered by soil. Under it, bones can survive for hundreds of years. They contain calcium which gives them hardness and strength.

Animal bones.

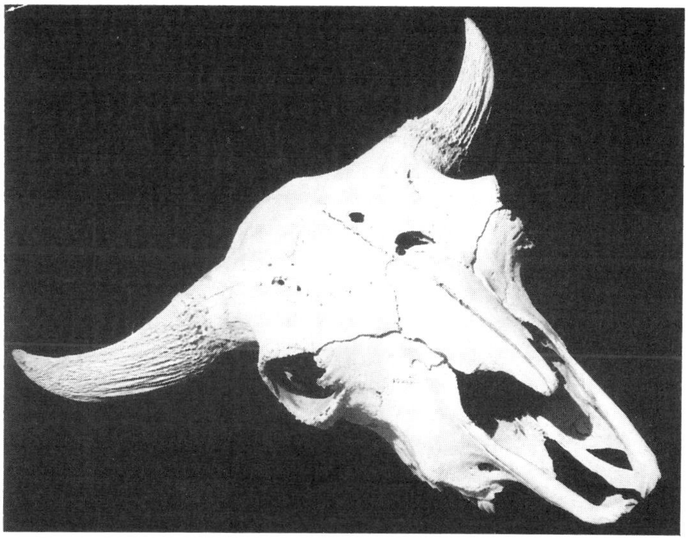

Pottery

Pottery pieces.

Most families owned at least one pottery bowl or dish. Sooner or later, these were broken and thrown away. If **archaeologists** dig them up, it could be another clue that a farm or village once stood nearby.

Activities

1 In your own words explain the meaning of these words: ridge and furrow, archaeologist.

2 Look at source B. It shows the site of a Norman village. From this list, write down what you think the numbers were: open fields; fish ponds; a road; a factory; a cinema.

3 Choose two from this list: pollen grains; animal bones; pottery. Explain how they can be useful to a historian.

4 Make a list of 10 things in your classroom which people might find a thousand years from now. Pick 5, and draw each in turn. Beside each one, explain what a historian would learn from it about people today.

14 Home Life

A *Building a villein's house.*

Home, for a villein and his wife, was a small one-roomed hut. It had a wooden frame and a thatched roof. In this one room they lived, ate and slept.

Houses like this were quick and easy to build but they were not perfect. They caught fire easily and could blow down in high winds. They were not very strong and people who leaned against the walls risked falling through them.

In the middle of the floor was the fire. Most of the time the house was very smoky and the walls were black with soot.

It was also very smelly, especially in winter. Then, the villein brought the family's animals into the house. They lived in a shed at the end of the room.

There wasn't much furniture. Perhaps a wooden table and stools to sit on, and a box to keep clothes in. Like the wooden dishes and plates that they ate from, it was all home-made.

An iron pot hung over the fire, and in this the wife cooked the family meals. Whenever possible, the cooking was done outside. It was so difficult to get rid of smoke and cooking smells inside the house.

If there was enough food they ate three meals a day. Breakfast was the first at 6 a.m. The family might own a cow so the youngest children had milk to drink. They ate a piece of coarse black bread to go with it. Their parents ate their bread with ale instead of milk.

At 10 a.m. they had more bread for dinner. This time they ate it with cheese or eggs. Supper was the main meal of the day at about 4 p.m. After working in the fields all day, the villein and his wife would be very hungry.

Sometimes there wasn't much to eat. Just a vegetable stew and more black bread. They used knives and spoons to eat with. They did not have forks. If they were lucky they had meat in the stew. It was usually bacon because pigs were easier to keep. The meat was fresh in autumn because this was when the pigs were killed.

The family did not eat all the meat though. There had to be enough for winter, so they smoked or salted it.

B *A villein and his fire.*

Meat preserved in this way was tough and took a lot of chewing. And even when it was boiled, it was always very salty. Sometimes the family had fish to eat. But only if they got permission from the local lord to fish in his river.

The fat left over from cooking was carefully collected. Reeds could be dipped in it and lit to make candles. They did not give off much light and usually the family went to bed when it was dark.

They slept on beds of straw and covered themselves with rugs. In winter it was so cold that they slept in their working clothes. Then they were grateful for the warmth given off by their animals at the other end of the room.

As soon as it was light the family got up. They washed in a tub of cold water. There was no bathroom and their lavatory was a stinking ditch outside called a midden.

C *Farm workers in the 1850s.*

Activities

1 Write sentences to explain these words: wattle; daub; midden; villein.

2 Look at source A and source C. Some of these statements are true, others are not. Write down the true ones, then explain what is wrong with the others.

(a) Villeins houses were very different from the houses of farm workers in the 1850s.
(b) The houses of the villeins and the farm workers were quick and cheap to build.
(c) Source C proves that farm workers in the 1850s had bigger families than the villeins.

3 Which of the three pictures is a primary source for our knowledge of Norman England? Explain how you decided.

15 Women in Norman Times

Women in Norman times led very different lives from women today. It did not matter if they were rich or poor. They were not free to do what they liked.

If a girl had rich parents, she could not choose the man she wanted to marry. Her parents did it for her. Some girls had to get married at the age of ten to men they had never seen before. Peasant girls were not much better off. They had to ask their lord's permission before they could marry a man from another manor.

In church, women learnt how God made the first man and women. Priests told them about Adam. Then how God had made Eve from one of Adam's ribs. They heard how wickedness came into the world after Eve was made.

Because of this, women were taught to believe that men were better than them. And men had to be obeyed. One man told his wife to copy the behaviour of a dog which always has its eyes on its owner.

It was a woman's job to look after children and do the housework. A peasant woman also had to make the family clothes. She had to spin the wool herself round a wooden tool called a distaff.

They still had to earn a living, though. Many did it by spinning wool. So many, in fact, that today we still use the word 'spinster' to describe a single woman.

A *Spinning and weaving wool.*

B *Nursing the sick.*

Peasant women always did the cooking. They nursed their children when they were sick and used remedies that their mothers and grandmothers had taught them. Often the remedies did not work and one child in three died before its first birthday.

If a boy died, the woman was expected to give birth to another as soon as possible. People thought boys were more useful than girls. They were supposed to do more of the hard work in the fields.

Yet even there, peasant women shared the work with their husbands. They milked the cows, cut the corn and dug up the vegetables.

These were men's jobs, done just as well by women. But men did not dream of doing jobs in the home. This was woman's work.

Life was normally easier for the wife of a rich baron. Servants did most of the work. However, if her husband was away, she had the job of defending the castle. And there are many stories where a baron's wife held out against attacks by enemy soldiers.

A wife was expected to be quiet and polite and ask her husband before making any decision. Most men assumed that women would always behave like this. And today, many men still assume that women will behave in certain ways.

Peasant girls did not have an education. Very few of them could read. Fewer still could write. And because of this we cannot find out what women thought about their lives. The sources in this chapter only tell us what men thought about them.

Apart from this, there is another problem for historians. Very little was written about women in Norman times. Source C and source F show what people in the 1450s thought about them. But their opinions are probably similar to the opinions of people who lived hundreds of years before them, like the writer of source E.

C *Peter Lombard wrote this about women around 1450.*

God did not make woman from Adam's head, because she was not intended to be his ruler. Nor from his feet, because she was not intended to be his slave. God made her from his side, because he wanted her to be his companion and friend.

D *Woman milking a cow.*

E *From the* Works and Days *by Hesiod who lived in Greece around 750 BC.*

First, get a house, a woman and an ox for ploughing. Let the woman be a slave, unmarried, who can help you in the field.

F *An Italian writer described the ideal wife in 1450.*

The most useful thing in a house is a wife ... When the woman sees anything to be done, she is ready to do it. She suffers in giving birth to her children and works hard to take care of them. She tires herself to look after her husband.

He then described a man without a wife.

On the floor in the room where he eats lie rinds, bones and rubbish, all left there without ever being swept up. The plates he washes as little as possible and the dog licks and cleans them. The pots are all greasy. And do you know how he lives? Like an animal.

Activities

1 Look at the women in source A. How have women's fashions changed since then?

2 a) Look at source B and source D.
b) Describe what is happening in source B.
c) Do you think nursing is a woman's job?
d) Is milking a cow a woman's job?
Explain your answers.

3 a) Read source F. Make a list of the jobs that this writer thought that women should do.
b) Does this writer think that a man is better or worse off without a wife? Give reasons.

4 a) Read source C. According to this writer, did God make women to be better than men, to be worse than men or to be equal to them? Explain your answer.
b) Do you agree with this writer? Give reasons.

5 Read source E. Do you think a man or a woman would give this advice? Explain your answer.

16 Towns in Norman England

Today most people live in towns. This wasn't the case in Norman times. Over a hundred towns are listed in the Domesday Book, but most of them were very small. Only London had a population over 10,000. The other towns were not much bigger than modern villages.

Some towns started next to a castle because people knew they would be protected there. Other people lived near monasteries hoping to get work from the monks, so more towns started.

Each town was built on land that belonged to the king or to a lord. The townspeople had to pay taxes to the lord, or work in his fields. In return, he agreed to protect them and many built walls around their towns to keep enemies out.

In most towns, shops selling the same type of goods were all on one street. At the same time as tailors were making clothes in Threadneedle Street, corn was on sale at Corn Hill and meat in Cheapside.

Usually the shop was just the front room of a tradesman's house. Instead of a large shop window they had wooden shutters. These could be let down to make a counter. Behind this was a workroom where the tradesman made the things that he sold.

Outside each shop was a picture sign which showed what was for sale. From these signs people could tell which street they were in. None of the streets had name plates because very few people could read.

People moved into the towns because they knew they could buy and sell what they wanted. As towns got bigger, people got richer. The richest of them all was the lord who owned the town. People were still forced to work on his land. Now he made them pay higher taxes.

Townspeople wanted to be free of these duties. They wanted to collect their own taxes and run towns their own way. Local lords saw in this a way of making much more money. They allowed people to buy these rights from them, and they were written down in a **charter**. In source B, you can read some of the rights that Henry II gave to the people of Nottingham.

A *Shopping in Norman times.*

B *Henry II's charter for Nottingham. It does not exist today but probably granted these rights:*

By the grace of God, Henry King of England greets you the people of Nottingham.

Know ye that I have granted to the people of Nottingham all those customs that they had in the time of my grandfather.

1 The right of **toll** which allows the people to take tolls from traders who enter the town.
2 The right of theam which allows people to control the courts and keep any fines.
3 The right to hold a market on Saturdays.
4 Freedom for any man who lives in the town for a year and a day without being claimed by his overlord.

And whoever lives in the town should pay taxes to the sum of £150.

Signed this day
Henry II

C *In 1190, Jews were murdered in London and towns throughout England. In 1192, a Jew wrote this about London.*

If you come to London, you should quickly pass through it as this city greatly displeases me. People from all countries live there in great numbers. They have brought to the city their bad habits and bad manners. Wicked men do well there. Avoid gambling, the theatre and the tavern. You will find druggists, fortune tellers, thieves, magicians and beggars. They live in every house.

D *Norman street sign.*

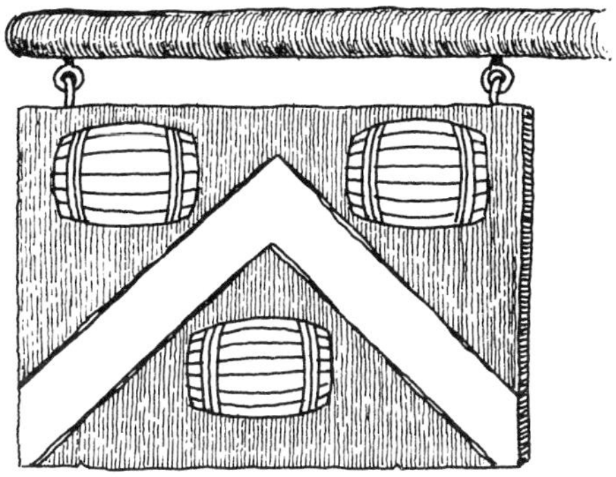

Activities

1 a) Look at source A. Which of these building materials would have been used to build these shops: wood; concrete; plastic; glass; steel; thatch; brick?
b) Make a list of the differences you can see between these shops and modern ones.

2 a) If you saw source D, what would you expect to be on sale nearby?
b) Sketch and label the street signs that you think you would have seen outside the shops in Fisher Street, Potters Gate, Tailors Row.

3 a) Read source C. Does this writer think that London is a good place to live, or not? Give reasons.
b) What reason might this man have had for being biased against London people?

4 a) Why did Norman kings let towns have charters?
b) Make your own copy of the charter on a piece of paper. You can make it appear old by first soaking the paper in tea or coffee, and then carefully drying it in an oven.

17 Crime and Punishment

William Rufus was crowned king in 1087. Like his father, William I, he allowed English people to keep their own laws. And their own ways of solving crime.

When someone was accused of breaking the law, they could ask local people to swear an oath that they were innocent. These people had to say the same set of words. If anyone made a mistake, this was God's way of showing that the accused person was guilty.

More serious crimes were solved by the ordeal. These were tests with water or hot iron. The Normans also brought a new type of ordeal to England – trial by battle.

A *Trial by battle – a fight between an accused man and his accuser.*

B *The punishment for many crimes was death.*

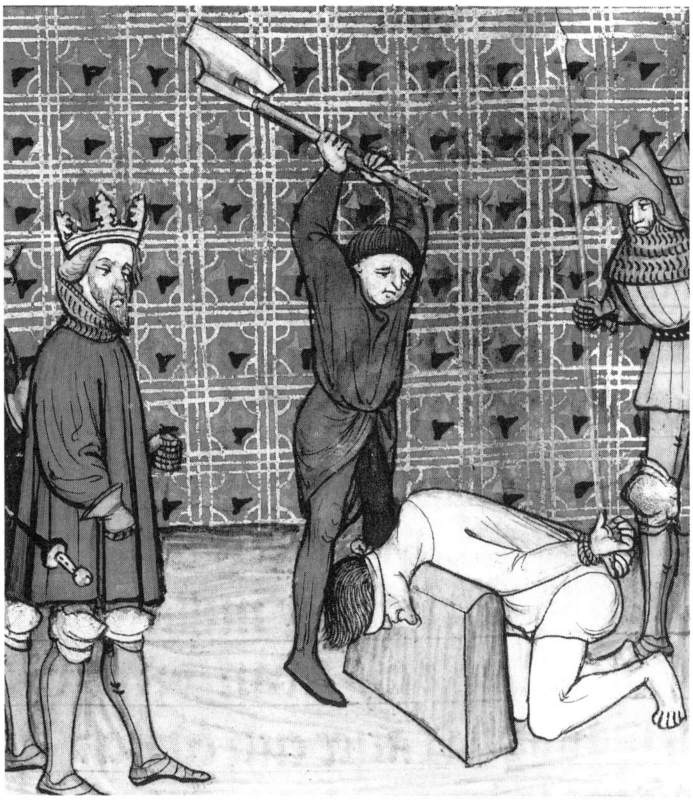

According to some Norman writers, William challenged Harold to this ordeal before the Battle of Hastings. They say that Harold refused.

To make sure that laws were obeyed, people were put into groups of ten called tithings. Each group had a leader. If one of his group did something wrong, he had to report them. If he didn't, the whole group was fined.

But punishments could be much more severe. Anyone caught hunting in the king's forests with a bow and arrow would have their fingers cut off. If you were guilty of murder you were executed. Men were hung and women burnt.

C *An account of the trial of Earl Waltheof, an English nobleman. He was accused of knowing about the plans of some other nobles to revolt against King William. It was written by Oderic Vitalis in about 1135.*

Earl Waltheof was summoned before the king. On the evidence of his wife Judith, he was accused of **treason**. Without fear, the earl said that the nobles had told him about their plans. But he said he had refused to take part in such wickedness.

After his confession there was a lot of discussion about the sentence he should get. There was a great difference of opinion amongst the members of the court. And because of this, they put off their decision for a whole year.

Meanwhile the earl was kept in the king's prison at Winchester. He was tall and very handsome and was a kind friend to the poor. His own people waited anxiously for him to be set free.

At last his enemies got together in such numbers that they formed the majority. They had their way and he was sentenced to death. There was no delay because the Normans were worried that the earl might escape. They were also greedy to get his land. He was therefore hurried at dawn, while the people were still asleep, to St Giles Hill.

There he threw himself on the ground and prayed to God. The executioners said to him, 'Get up so we can carry out the king's orders.' He replied, 'Wait awhile until I have said the Lord's Prayer.' They agreed but when he came to the last sentence his sobbings became so violent that he could not finish the prayer.

The executioner waited no longer. He drew his sword and cut off the earl's head in a single stroke. But the head, after it was cut off, said in a clear voice, 'But deliver us from evil. Amen.'

His body was then thrown into a hole dug on the spot and covered with green turf.

Trials by ordeal.

People who sold rotten food were put in the stocks. Townspeople could then throw the food back at them.

Activities

1 a) Draw the pictures which show trials by ordeal.
b) From the list below, write out the correct caption underneath each picture.

If the arm had started to heal after three days God had done this and the person was innocent.
If the person sank they were innocent. If they floated, God had rejected them and they were guilty.
If the hand had not started to heal after three days the accused was guilty.

c) Why do you think the Norman writers say that Harold refused to fight William?

2 a) Do you think the tithings were a good way to make people obey the law? Give reasons.
b) Why would people caught hunting with a bow and arrow have their fingers cut off?

3 a) Read source C. Do you think Earl Waltheof had a fair trial, or not? Explain your answer.
b) Is this writer biased in favour of Earl Waltheof, or against him? Give reasons.

18 Curing Illness and Disease

If you are ill today, you can go to a doctor or a hospital to be treated. For most people in Norman times this wasn't possible. Only the rich could afford to pay for doctors. But their treatments could be very painful and often did not work.

Doctors thought that people sometimes became ill when they had too much blood in their body. Their cure was to take some of it out. They did this either by cutting into an artery, or by placing blood-sucking leeches all over the body.

Doctors had more success in treating wounds. They could practise on soldiers who were hurt in battle. Their main form of treatment was cauterising. This meant putting a red hot poker on to the wound.

If the patient didn't die of shock first, there was a good chance of surviving. There were no **anaesthetics**, but cauterising did clean the wound and stop the bleeding.

The Church did not encourage people to become doctors. Priests taught that sickness and disease were punishments from God. You became ill when you were sinful. So the only cure was to lead a better life. If you did, God would make you better, not a doctor.

A *A doctor and his patient – extracting an arrow.*

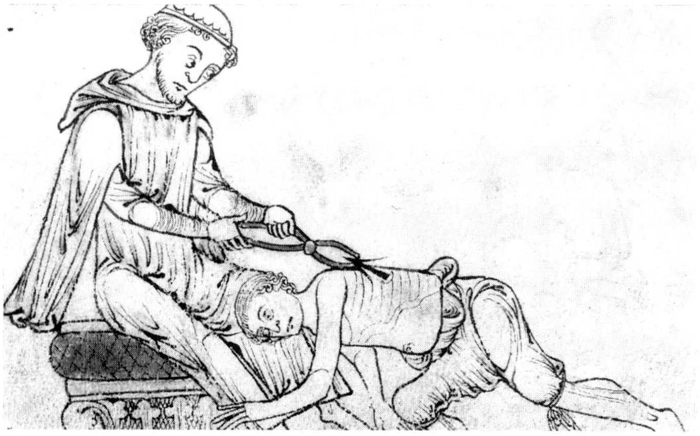

Any sick traveller could expect to be looked after at a monastery. Here the monks were allowed to treat people with herbs grown in the monastery garden. Today these herbs are still used to make drugs and medicines.

Even the monks charged for their cures, so poor people had to find other remedies when they were ill. Some used magic spells and lucky charms. Other people drank spring water that had been blessed by saints. And everyone used the remedies they had learnt from their parents and grandparents.

Toothache could be treated by hanging a magpie's beak round your neck, headache by putting goat's cheese on your head.

B *Leprosy killed thousands of people in Norman times.*

One of the worst types of illness was leprosy. This was a very infectious skin disease, and thousands of people died from it. People who caught the disease were called lepers. They had to leave their home and family, to go and live with other lepers. Many never returned.

C *This shows the strict rules which lepers had to obey.*

First of all, the leper must stay in his house. Then he should be told that a priest is on his way to take him to church. The priest then speaks to him with kind words. When he has sprinkled him with holy water, the priest with his cross in front of him leads the leper to church.

Inside the church, a black cloth should be put on to a table away from the altar. The sick man should take his place on bended knees underneath the table, being like a dead man. In this position the man hears **mass**. With a spade the priest throws soil onto his feet saying, 'You are dead to the world, but alive again with God.'

When he leaves the church the priest sprinkles him with more holy water. The priest must then say the following words: 'I forbid you to enter churches or to go into a market or into any groups of people. Also I forbid you ever to wash your hands or any of your belongings in any stream of water. If you are thirsty you must drink water from your own cup.

Also I forbid you ever to go out without your leper's cloak so that other people can recognise you. I forbid you, wherever you are, to touch anything that you want to buy. When you are on a journey never go through a narrow lane because you might meet someone. If you need to go over rough ground, you must never touch posts to help you cross, until you have put your gloves on.

From now on I forbid you to eat or drink with anyone except lepers. And when you die you will be buried in your own house, and not in church.'

D *An ointment for the skin, 1290.*

I collected a good number of those beetles which in summer are found in the dung of oxen. Also some crickets which sing in the fields. I cut off the heads and wings of the crickets and put them with the beetles and some oil into a pot. I covered it, and left it afterwards for a day and a night in a bread oven. I drew out the pot and heated it on the fire, pounded the ingredients and rubbed them into the sick parts. In three days the pain had gone.

A skull operation.

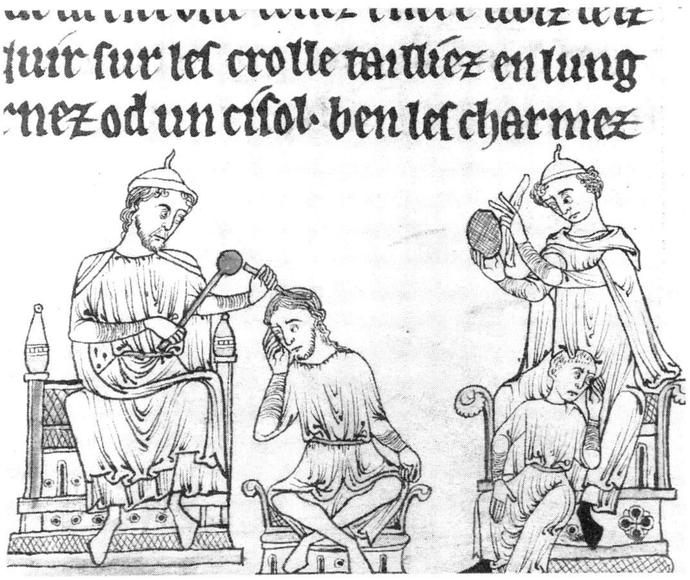

Activities

1 Here are two statements which describe what the Normans knew about medicine and disease. Explain whether they are true or false.

They did not think that infectious diseases could be stopped by keeping sick people away from healthy ones.
They did not think that cauterising could clean a wound.

2 a) Look at source A. Describe what is happening in the picture.
b) What differences can you see between this scene and an operation in a hospital today?

3 a) Look at source B. Can you think of any reason why lepers had to carry bells with them?
b) What signs are there that this man has leprosy?

4 You are a leper. Describe the priest's visit to your house and explain what it is like to have the disease.

5 Read source D, then write out your own cure for a skin infection.

19 The White Ship Disaster, 1120

William Rufus died in a hunting accident in 1100. Henry, who was William the Conqueror's youngest son, became king. He married an English noblewoman and they had two children. Like his father, Henry spent a lot of his time in Normandy. And, when he was away from England, Henry often took his children with him on his journey.

His son William was with him when he visited Normandy in 1120. He was only seventeen years old but Henry had already chosen him to be the next king. That was, until the winter's night when they sailed back to England.

A *The White Ship disaster, from a 19th century picture.*

B *William of Malmesbury wrote this account in about 1125.*

On 25th November the king set sail for England just before nightfall. But his son ordered that another ship should be prepared for himself and the other young nobles. The sailors, who had drunk too much, shouted out that they would overtake the king's ship which had already set out.

These reckless youths, now drunk with wine, launched their ship even though it was now dark. The ship flew swifter than an arrow across the waves. But the drunken crew was careless and drove it onto a rock not far from the shore.

Everyone rushed on deck shouting and crying.

They got their boathooks ready to try and push the ship off the rocks. Then the waves washed some of the crew overboard. Water got in through holes in the side and drowned others.

At last, another boat was launched and the young prince was rescued. He would have got to the shore safely if his sister hadn't begged him to save her.

He ordered his boat to return so he could rescue her. But so many people leapt into the boat that it capsized and sank. Only one person survived until morning to tell the story.

The disaster was made worse because of the difficulty of finding the bodies. They became food for the monsters of the deep.

C *Oderic Vitalis wrote this account in about 1135.*

Before the king set sail he spoke to a man called Thomas. This man said to the king, 'When your father sailed across the sea to fight Harold my father took him in his ship. I would like to do the same for you. I have a boat called the White Ship which is all ready for you.'

The king replied, 'I have already chosen a ship which suits me, but I will let you take my sons, William and Richard.'

The sailors were very happy at hearing this news. They greeted William and asked him to give them something to drink. As soon as the wine was brought to them they all had a big drinking match and got drunk.

There were 300 people on board ship. But some of them got off when they saw it was overcrowded with drunken youths. Apart from the king's treasure and some crates of wine there was no cargo on board. It was full of passengers.

Thomas was foolish and recklessly boasted that he would soon leave behind him all the other ships. The sailors grabbed the oars and put up the sails. They made the ship rush through the water at a great speed.

But Thomas steered without thinking and took the White Ship off course. Its right bow crashed into a huge rock. Two planks were shattered and the ship filled with water.

The passengers and crew cried out but their shouts were soon stopped by the waves. They all drowned together, except two men called Berold and Geoffrey who hung onto the mast.

After his first plunge into the sea, Thomas recovered his senses. He saw the two men and shouted out, 'What has happened to the king's son?' They told him that he and everyone who was with him had drowned. He said, 'I cannot live any longer,' and let himself sink under the waves in total despair. He preferred to drown rather than face the king's anger.

The night was bitterly cold and frosty and the young Geoffrey lost his strength. He fell into the sea and disappeared. Berold survived until dawn the next day.

In the morning three fishermen took him into their boat and back to the shore. There he told his sad story to a crowd of people.

Drunken passengers go on board.

People said that after hearing that his children had drowned, Henry never smiled again.

Activities

1 For each source, write down whether it is primary or secondary. Give reasons.

2 a) Look at source A. Explain which part of the story you think it shows.
b) Where do you think the artist got his information from?

3 a) What information does source B give about Prince William's death that source C does not?
b) If these writers had wanted to check the story of Prince William's voyage, whom could they have asked?
c) Who do you think was to blame for the shipwreck? Give reasons.

4 A film company has asked you to make a film about the shipwreck. First you must draw a storyboard. This will tell the story of the shipwreck in a set of 10 pictures, like a cartoon strip. It will start with King Henry speaking to the owner of the White Ship and end at the moment he is told that his children are dead. Use sources B and C to help you.

20 The York Massacre, 1190

At this moment, you are probably sitting in a classroom. Around you are people you have known for some time. Some of them will be friends of yours, some might not be. But in many ways, you will be different from them.

Your height, the length of your hair, the colour of your eyes and skin are things that make you different. You might have been born in a town or country far from where your friends were born. Perhaps you believe in a different religion.

All people are different, but today we have laws that treat everyone the same way. This hasn't always been the case. In Norman times, it could be very dangerous to be different from other people, as Jewish people knew well.

For years, the Jews had lived peacefully in France. Then, in 1066, William the Conqueror allowed some Jewish families to live in England. They made their first homes in London. They lived closely together because they did not know any of the local people.

A *A Jewish man painted in 1277.*

The Jews were starting life in a strange, new country. They spoke a different language and believed in Judaism – a religion which most people in England did not understand. They found it hard to get jobs because the **guilds** only took on people who were Christians. Instead, many Jews made their living by lending money.

B *A receipt made out by a Jewish moneylender, 15th November 1182.*

To all persons seeing this deed. Know that I have received from Richard Malebysse £4 of the debt he owes to my master Aaron. This is out of the great debt which he owes to my master. I have given him a day for settlement.

Their lives changed for the worse with the **Crusades**. Muslims had attacked the Holy Land, the place where Jesus had lived. People in England and France were very angry about this.

Many of them went on Crusades to fight the **Muslims**. They remembered their Bible stories which told them about the good things that Jesus had done. They also remembered the way he had died and the people who had killed him – the Jews.

Other people had different reasons for disliking the Jews. They had borrowed money and now couldn't pay it back. In 1189, Jews were attacked in London. Others were beaten up in Lincoln. But it was the Jews in York who suffered most. Their houses were burgled and set on fire. Some people were burnt alive.

The Jews were very frightened. Many left their houses and hurried to the castle. Locked behind the castle gates, they thought they were safe. They asked the sheriff to help them, but he told them they should not have taken over the castle. He ordered the people of York to get them out.

C *At the end of the 12th century, William of Newburgh described what happened next:*

The Jews held back the enemy with stones taken from the wall. But when the siege machines were brought into position, the taking of the castle became certain. The Jews were brave, but they were in despair, and had little sleep discussing what they should do.

Yomtob, their leader, told them they had two choices:
1 They could open the castle gates and ask the people for mercy Then they would be baptised and forced to live as Christians. Some of the Jews decided to do this.
2 They could kill themselves.

William of Newburgh continues the story:
The Jews made a fire and burnt their most precious possessions, everything they could. When this was done and the roof was set alight, they prepared their throats for the sacrifice. Joce (one of their leaders) cut the throat of Anna, his wife, and did not spare his own sons. Then, this was done by the other men. All of them were killed together. Those who had chosen to live tried to put out the fire lit by their friends.

At daybreak, crowds of people gathered to storm the castle. Those Jews who were left stood on the gates and told the crowd about the slaughter of their people. They threw down their dead bodies as proof of the sacrifice.

When they said this with tears, many of our men were horrified. But the leaders of the crowd, among whom was a certain Richard Malebysse, did not pity them. They spoke fair words to them so they would come out. But when they did so they seized them as enemies and butchered them.

The York Massacre.

D *The Jews locked themselves into this castle, now rebuilt and called Clifford's Tower.*

Activities

1 a) Write out the words which you think best describe the man in source A: good-looking; mean; honest; ugly; kind; lazy; greedy; cruel; smiling; brave.
b) Overall, does it give a good or bad impression of the man? Explain why.
c) Why do you think the artist has painted the man's side view?
d) Why might the artist decide to paint a picture of an ugly Jew rather than a good-looking one?
e) Draw the man's face from the front and put a smile on him. Now, describe your picture.

2 a) Look at source B. How much money had Richard Malebysse paid back to Aaron the moneylender?
b) Why is source B useful to a historian in explaining why the York massacre took place?

3 You are a newspaper reporter. You have been asked to write a report about the massacre. Think of a headline, and then in your own words explain what happened.

21 Normans and English

William I and an English noble.

The Normans weren't the first people to invade England. In 1066, they were the latest in a long line of people. Years before them, the Angles and Saxons had invaded from Germany. Later on, *they* were attacked by the Vikings who sailed over from Norway and Denmark.

These groups of people stayed and made new lives for themselves in England. In many ways they were very different from each other. They had their own language and religion and even looked different.

But over the years they forgot their differences. It was these people that William fought against, and then ruled over as King of England.

William brought with him about 10,000 Normans. For the first few years people hated them. They were easy to spot because their hair was cut short and shaved at the back. They didn't have beards and they wore longer clothes than the English.

Hundreds were killed after the invasion. So many, in fact, that William charged the English a murder fine. Whenever a Norman was murdered, the people who lived on the nearest manor had to pay, on top of all the other taxes, and the murders soon stopped.

At first the Normans and English could not understand each other. The Normans spoke French, the English did not. This made the king's job more difficult. He had to make people obey him and so he made new laws in English.

At the same time, people in England started to learn new French words like beef and bacon. They also began to use French sounds like *oy* in their words. Today this sound is sometimes spelt *oi*, and you can hear it in the words choice, noise and joy.

The Normans changed English laws as well. After the invasion, juries of local people were allowed to help judges decide in court cases. This gave anyone accused of a crime the chance of a fairer trial.

For the wives of the dead English nobles, life was also different. Many re-married after the Battle of Hastings, some of them to Norman barons. Their children learnt French and English. They grew up knowing what it was like to be English and a Norman as well.

Boys were christened with new first names like Richard, Thomas or William. For the first time too they had surnames. They might be called after the village or manor that their father owned. Or they might simply be called Norman. English people gradually copied this idea and today everyone has a surname.

In time, the English and the Normans forgot their differences and settled down together. They married into each other's families and copied each other's fashions. Soon it was impossible to tell who were the Normans and who were the English.

The Normans came to this country from overseas. Over the years millions of people have done the same. Today, they all call themselves British, and live alongside all the other people who have made Britain their home.

A *William of Malmesbury had an English mother and a Norman father. He wrote this about English people early in the 12th century.*

At this time (1066), the English wore short clothes that reached to the knee. They trimmed their beards, wore gold bracelets on their arms and had tattoos on their skin. They used to overeat and drink till they were sick. The English gave these habits to their conquerors.

B *A 12th century miracle quoted in* The Story of English *by Robert McCrum, 1986.*

A friend of St Wulfric of Haselbury, a certain Brother William, laid hands on a dumb man who had been brought to him. At once the man could speak both English and French. The local parish priest, Brichtric, complained that this was unfair. He had served the Church faithfully for many years and yet Brother William had made it possible for a total stranger to speak two languages while he, Brichtric, had to remain dumb in the presence of his bishop. Though he was a priest, Brichtric knew little or no Latin, and no French.

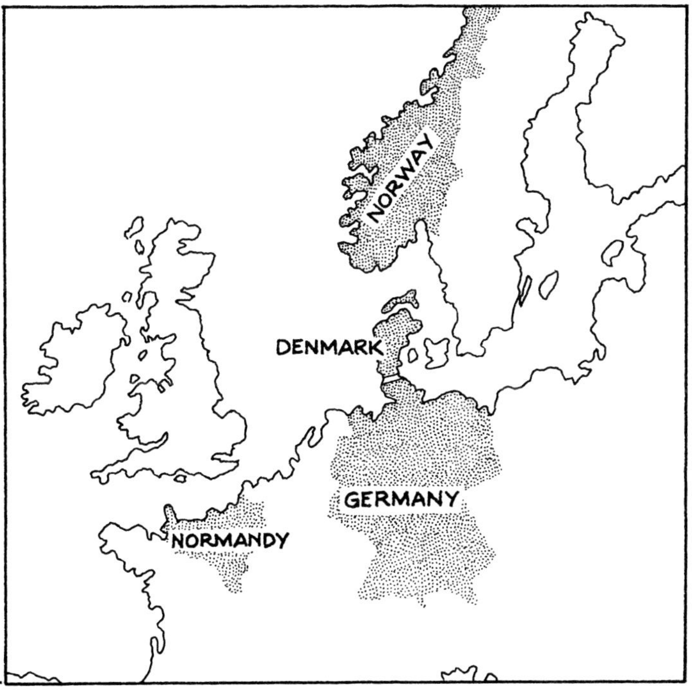

Activities

1 a) Match up the people on the left with the countries they came from on the right.

Normans	Germany
Vikings	Normandy
Angles and Saxons	Norway and Denmark

b) Copy the map into your book. Draw arrows on it to show where these people came from when they invaded England.

2 a) Explain what the murder fine was.
b) Why do you think it was not collected after 1300?

3 Make a list of ten words which have the *oi* or *oy* sound in them.

4 a) Look at the picture on p. 44. Which man is English?
b) How is he different from the Normans in the picture? Use source A to help you.

5 a) Read source B. What was Brichtric complaining about?
b) Does this source suggest that:

1 It was important for people in Norman times to know both French and English.
2 It was not important for people to know both French and English?

Explain your answer.

Revision

1 This square includes some hidden words. They are all words which appear in the glossary. They could read up, down or sideways. Each time you find a word, write it down and write a sentence about it.

D	A	S	O	U	R	C	E
M	N	Q	R	S	D	M	F
O	A	T	H	I	L	O	T
V	I	L	L	E	I	N	O
T	R	E	V	G	U	K	B
N	O	B	L	E	G	X	B
T	U	B	A	R	O	N	A

2 Read this source.

William held his forces when they turned to run, gave them courage and shared their danger. He was more often heard shouting to them to follow him, than ordering them to go on ahead. At the mere sight of this wonderful knight, his enemies lost heart even before they received a scratch.

a) What questions would you need to ask about this source before you could believe it was true?
b) Why do you need to ask these questions?

3 Copy this list. Next to each source explain whether it is primary or secondary and give reasons.

The Bayeux Tapestry, the Domesday Book, a Norman church, 'William the Conqueror,' – a film made in 1986.

This 19th century picture shows a scene from the Battle of Hastings.

4 a) Describe what you think is happening in the painting above.
b) What evidence would you need to prove that the event shown here actually happened? Give reasons.

5 This is the site of a Norman castle. Write down the letters A, B and C. Beside each one, write the correct name for that part of the castle.

12th century motte and bailey castle at Pleshey in Essex.

Glossary

abbot head monk of a monastery or abbey
acre area of land, about half a hectare
anaesthetic drug given before an operation to put a patient to sleep
archaeologist person who studies historical remains, which sometimes have to be dug up from the ground
baron important Norman nobleman
bishop chief clergyman in a group of villages or towns
bracken plant found on moorland or hillsides
chapter room in a monastery where meetings were held
charter written agreement between a lord and townspeople
chronicle book about historical events
Crusades holy wars in which Christians went to fight Muslims
evidence clues which historians can study to try and work out what happened in the past
famine terrible shortage of food
guild group of craftsmen who work in the same trade, e.g. the Tailors Guild
hectare area of land about the size of a football pitch
hermit person who lives alone, perhaps in a cave or in the mountains
hide area of land, about 12 hectares
hostage person who is held prisoner and only freed when certain promises are kept
mass Catholic church service
merchant person who sells things to other people
monastery building where monks live
monk religious man who spends his life in a monastery
Muslims people who believe in the Islamic religion
noble important English lord or lady
oath solemn promise
parchment animal skin used for writing on
porter person who opened and closed a castle gate
priest clergyman in the Catholic church
ransom money paid to kidnappers to free hostages
rebel person who fights against a king or ruler
revolt uprising by people against a king or ruler
sheriff an official who kept the law in a county
siege an attack on a castle or walled town that could last for many days
source anything that gives information about the past
tapestry picture made from wool woven on linen
tax money paid by the people to the king or ruler
toll a charge paid by people who use a market, road or bridge
treason a crime against the king or country
villein a peasant farmer who did not own any land

Index